GIVE ME A
Minute!

ONE MINUTE MESSAGES TO PRAY, PREPARE, AND PERSIST UNTIL SOMETHING HAPPENS

A Compilation By Best-Selling Author
ALLISON DENISE ARNETT

BRAND IT BEAUTIFULLY™ · HOUSTON

Give Me a Minute

Unless otherwise notated, scripture quotations are taken from the Holy Bible, New Living Translation, copyright ©1996, 2004, 2015 by Tyndale House Foundation. Used by permission of Tyndale House Publishers, Carol Stream, Illinois 60188. All rights reserved.

ISBN: 978-1-7354763-4-6 (Hardcover Edition)

Printed and bound in the United States of America

Book Designed and Published by Brand It Beautifully™
www.branditbeautifully.com
allison@imallisondenise.com

FOR ADDITIONAL MEDITATIONS &
LESSONS CONNECT WITH THE

Visionary & Publisher's

FAITH BENEATH THE CROWN™
PODCAST ON ITUNES & SPOTIFY

Contents

Section One: PRAY

Section Two: PLAN & PREPARE

Contents (cont.)

Section Three: PERSIST

To every Christian leader brave enough to admit that sometimes we just need a minute to pray, prepare, or be reminded to persist.

INTRODUCTION

If your actions inspire others to dream more, learn more, do more, and become more – you are a leader. ~ John Quincy Adams

Whether in your home, the office, your community, your ministry or otherwise, if you inspire others to more, you are a leader. While being a leader often comes with accolades and benefits, it can also come with overwhelm, confusion, and pressure. It is in these moments where true leaders are developed. Will you fold under pressure? Will you give in to the overwhelm? Will you circle in confusion? Or will you give yourself grace and remember that you are just as human as the people you inspire and lead?

Since you are reading this, it would appear that you are the type of leader that understands you don't have all the answers and are self-aware enough to recognize when a shift needs to take place. The shift from leading to following. Following the example of God who, after working and creating for six days, took some time to rest. Or Jesus who would often retreat to a quiet place to pray and who pressed forward in His assignment despite hitting a rough patch or two.

Give Me a Minute is designed to be a resting place, a praying place, and a renewing place. Take it minute by minute; in whatever order God leads you. Repeat a minute if you need to. Just find what you need to reset and restart.

In each section you will find:

- Mindfulness activities you can complete in 2 minutes or less
- 1-minute motivational messages to pray, prepare, or persist
- Journal pages to write out your thoughts or action steps
- Coloring pages to calm your mind and spirit. Color pencils will probably work best for these.

Complete one or all when you start your day, in the middle of your day, or to end your day... whenever you need a minute.

To stay centered as a leader and keep God at the center of all we do, we must take time to

Pray

TAKE A
DEEP
BREATH IN
and release

Take a minute with
ALLISON DENISE ARNETT

Ask for help not because you are weak, but because you want to remain strong. ~ Les Brown

When you have a connection with someone, you two are in alignment with each other and can share things openly with each other. You might even do *anything* for that person. Well it's kind of like when Jesus said,

"If you remain in Me and My words remain in you [that is, if we are vitally united and My message lives in your heart], ask whatever you wish and it will be done for you." John 15:7 AMP

Do you have a connection with God? Do you feel vitally united with God? If not, take some time to connect. If yes, then ask for what you need! Ask according to His word, because He watches over His word to perform it. It is said, that we have not because we ask not. So right now you may need help. You may need strength. You may need a "yes". You may need clarity. Or a sweet vacation. Whatever it is... ask! Take everything to God in prayer.

Affirmation: I ask for what I need and since the Lord is my Shepherd, I shall not be found wanting.

What is your prayer for today?

_____

_____

_____

_____

_____

_____

_____

_____

_____

_____

_____

_____

_____

_____

_____

_____

_____

_____

_____

_____

_____

_____

_____

_____

IMAGINE THE LIFE YOU'VE BEEN
dreaming of

Take a minute with
CLARICE MAY CREGGER

Grow through what you go through. - Unknown

It can be hard to see the growth that we are making while going through the challenges we face, but know that you will grow with everything that you go through if you allow it. Plan and prepare, but keep God at the center of everything you do in your life, business, or ministry using prayer. Understand that you are growing like a plant and you have to allow yourself to bloom and to be uprooted from where you were so He can grow you. Seek God in prayer and ask Him to show you how to grow in your current situation.

Affirmation: I let go of control, let God be God, and trust in His timing.

What is your prayer for today?

_____

_____

_____

_____

_____

_____

_____

_____

_____

_____

_____

_____

_____

_____

_____

_____

_____

_____

_____

_____

_____

BLOOM
WHERE
YOU ARE
PLANTED

RELAX YOUR JAW AND NOW
your shoulders

Take a minute with
CLARISSA PRITCHETT

Prayer is the key to success. ~ Unknown

You are living your greatest purpose. You are at the pinnacle of your mountain and prayer is everything you need to continue climbing and pushing you to reach the top through every season of life. In the same way you feed your body daily with food, you should feed your spirit with prayer. Those who pray never fail. Prayer is what connects you to our All-Mighty God, fuels your faith, and gives you unlimited potential to persist. Prayer propels you to step out with confidence into greatness. Prayer is what helps you land with grace and ease when you fall and picks you back up to continue your climb. Pray daily with passion and nothing will prevent you from success. Pray and you will not be defeated. Pray and you will not be a victim or be afraid to pursue all God has called you to do. Go forth and pray, prepare, persist, and shine bright like God created you to do!

Affirmation: Every day I pray with passion to prepare, persist, and succeed in all God has called me to do.

What is your prayer for today?

_____

_____

_____

_____

_____

_____

_____

_____

_____

_____

_____

_____

_____

_____

_____

_____

_____

_____

_____

_____

_____

_____

_____

Get up

AND TAKE
A SHORT
WALK

Take a minute with
DEBORAH RIVERS DECOTEAU

Believe in what you pray for. ~ Unknown

You've been praying for it but do you really believe it can be yours? Do you really believe God wants to bless you? Or are you secretly, in your inner most thoughts and feelings, believing it can happen for everyone *except* you? Mark 11:24 reminds us that "*...all the things you pray and ask for - believe that you have received them, and you will have them.*" Perhaps the source of your stress today is that you wonder why it seems God has forgotten your blessings or that you don't fully trust that they are on the way. I encourage you to embody the belief that it is already yours and you will see the physical manifestation of it soon. Really settle into the feeling of having received it already. Live there. And before, during, and after praying – only believe.

Affirmation: I believe in what I pray for.

What is your prayer for today?

_____

_____

_____

_____

_____

_____

_____

_____

_____

_____

_____

_____

_____

_____

_____

_____

_____

_____

_____

_____

_____

_____

_____

FAVORED

BY GOD

Dance!

TO YOUR
FAVORITE
SONG

Take a minute with
JISELLE ALLEYNE-CLEMENT

He who dwells in the secret place of the Most High shall abide under the shadow of the almighty. ~ Psalm 91:1

Prayer offers you the ability to communicate in that specially coded language to your Heavenly Father. The beautiful thing is that He understands YOUR unique prayer language. He understands you on the days when you have many words, as well as the days when all you can articulate is a sigh and your tears become your words. Wherever you are in this moment, understand, that the potency of prayer comes from dwelling in the secret place with your Heavenly Father. Know that when you leave this place, your strength will be renewed. So today, create a permanent space in the secret place where you can speak freely and your Father listens attentively. He delights to hear your language of prayer.

Affirmation: I find my secret place and find the strength of my language of prayer.

What is your prayer for today?

_____
_____
_____
_____
_____
_____
_____
_____
_____
_____
_____
_____
_____
_____
_____
_____
_____
_____
_____
_____
_____
_____
_____
_____
_____
_____
_____

CALL SOMEONE SPECIAL FOR A QUICK

conversation

Take a minute with
DR. KAREN MAXFIELD-LUNKIN

However, this kind does not go out except by prayer and fasting. ~ Mathew 17: 21

Working in the ministry or marketplace we are often so focused on caring for others that we neglect to care for ourselves. Ignoring our own needs and the very human fact that we too need healing, deliverance, sometimes therapy, and frequent times of rest and rejuvenation – can leave us vulnerable when facing stressful situations. Consider preparing for these times with prayer and fasting. Through fasting, we enter a resting, self-cleansing process known as autophagy. Fasting is an excellent way to prepare for stressful times. When you know you have a particularly stressful meeting, conversation, or even the unexpected circumstances that life and business can bring; prepare by fasting. So yes, absolutely you must pray, and sometimes you must also couple fasting with your prayer to give yourself space to cleanse, strengthen, and rejuvenate.

Affirmation: I give myself space to cleanse, strengthen. and rejuvenate through fasting and prayer.

What is your prayer for today?

_____

_____

_____

_____

_____

_____

_____

_____

_____

_____

_____

_____

_____

_____

_____

_____

_____

_____

_____

_____

_____

REMEMBER

WHY

YOU

started

Take a minute with
KARYN THOMPSON FARMER

Trust in and rely confidently on the Lord with all your heart and do not rely on your own insight or understanding. ~ Proverbs 3:5

Give yourself some grace. You are a leader, but it is not your responsibility to have all the answers. However, you do need to know and spend time with the One who does. Here are a few prayer pointers to help you do this:

1. Establish your prayer room. Determine the location, atmosphere, and aroma.

2. Be intentional and consistent at all times.

3. Pray without ceasing.

4. Record your prayers and the Lord's answers to them.

5. Pray for those that are for you and, most importantly, pray for those that come up against you.

Affirmation: I trust in the Lord who has all the answers I need.

What is your prayer for today?

_____

_____

_____

_____

_____

_____

_____

_____

_____

_____

_____

_____

_____

_____

_____

_____

_____

_____

_____

_____

_____

BLESSED
& HIGHLY
FAVORED

RETREAT
TO A
QUIET
calm place

Take a minute with
NADIA MORALES

Then you will call on me and come and pray to me, and I will listen to you. ~ Jeremiah 29:12, NIV

As you face struggles head-on (and sometimes with your eyes closed), perhaps you may wish things could be easier. That the people around you would cut you some slack. For blessings to trickle down, so you can catch your breath as you run the hamster wheel of life.

You're tired. Maybe you feel alone too. You may be asking yourself many questions – "Am I enough?" "Am I doing the right thing?" "How do I move forward?"

This is an opportunity to spark a conversation with God. Instead of keeping things to yourself, I invite you to look at times of distress as an opportunity to grow in the Lord. Find comfort in His presence. Seek His will. Certainly, you will get the answers you seek.

Affirmation: Through prayer, I am filled with the Spirit of God that suffices me in times of distress.

What is your prayer for today?

_____

_____

_____

_____

_____

_____

_____

_____

_____

_____

_____

_____

_____

_____

_____

_____

_____

_____

_____

CRY IF YOU NEED TO

it's ok

Take a minute with
PATTI DENISE HENRY

See, I have this day set thee over the nations and over the kingdoms, to root out, and to pull down, and to destroy, and to throw down, to build, and to plant. ~ Jeremiah 1:10

You have answered the call to be an ambassador for Christ. To be a leader that accepts the responsibility of reconciling men unto God. Know that God hears you always when you pray and be confident in the fact that if you ask anything according to His will that He will hear you. He will hear your cry on behalf of yourself and the people to whom you are assigned. Say – *"Father, I trust You. I trust Your will. I trust Your way and I trust Your purpose for my life. Let everything I do and say, reflect Your character and that I walk not after the flesh but after the Spirit."*

Affirmation: I trust God's purpose for my life.

What is your prayer for today?

_____

_____

_____

_____

_____

_____

_____

_____

_____

_____

_____

_____

_____

_____

_____

_____

_____

_____

_____

_____

OPEN THE WINDOWS OF HEAVEN

Move!

THREE PARTS OF YOUR BODY

Take a minute with
RONDA PARKS

Rejoice always, pray without ceasing, give thanks in all circumstances; for this is the will of God in Christ Jesus for you. ~ 1 Thessalonians 5:16-18

When God awakens you in the morning, the first thing you should say is "Thank You," and then offer up a prayer. As you journey throughout your day, you may get to a place where you feel you need more prayer. The beauty of this is that God has given us the power to be able to pray and to have conversations with Him anytime and anywhere. There's no space that God cannot be reached. So in the middle of your day whenever it is, if you need to speak to God, call out to Him. Find a secret place or moment to pray in your closet, in your car, or wherever you can. God will answer your prayers. God knows your voice and will hear you. He will strengthen you through your prayer.

Affirmation: I find time and space to pray.

What is your prayer for today?

_____

_____

_____

_____

_____

_____

_____

_____

_____

_____

_____

_____

_____

_____

_____

_____

_____

_____

_____

_____

_____

_____

Faith without works is dead. You have prayed and should continue to pray, but now it is time to

Plan & Prepare

REMEMBER HOW WELL YOU'VE DONE

so far!

Take a minute with
ALLISON DENISE ARNETT

The best preparation for tomorrow is doing your best today. ~ Unknown

Yesterday is gone and tomorrow is not yet here. Today is all you have. What can you do today to make it easier for you to press through tomorrow? How can you set yourself up for success? For example, before preparing your best dish you purchase all the ingredients, pull out all the necessary dishes, set aside the appropriate amount of time, and maybe even put your recipe book on the counter. After preparation like this, you feel ready to begin the task. It feels less overwhelming. You can then accomplish the task with ease knowing that you have everything you need. So I encourage you to do something today that your tomorrow self will thank you for. Prepare for a great tomorrow by doing your best today.

Affirmation: I do my best and let God do the rest..

How will you prepare today?

_____

_____

_____

_____

_____

_____

_____

_____

_____

_____

_____

_____

_____

_____

_____

_____

_____

_____

_____

_____

DO A QUICK BRAIN DUMP
on paper

Take a minute with
CLARICE MAY CREGGER

Don't fret or be anxious. God's, got you. Rest on him. ~ Unknown

Don't worry about the past. Don't worry about the when's and the how's. There's freedom in living in the moment and taking life day by day. Be careful not to miss out on a perfectly divine moment just because you're so anxiously planning and preparing for the outcome you have in mind. Trust the process and put your best foot forward. Live one moment at a time. Relax and know that He entrusted you with this life, business, or ministry for a reason. Everything that He's planted in your heart rests on Him.

Affirmation: I let go of the anxiety of planning and preparing and embrace the ease of trusting God.

How will you prepare today?

_____

_____

_____

_____

_____

_____

_____

_____

_____

_____

_____

_____

_____

_____

_____

_____

_____

_____

_____

_____

_____

_____

PLAN SOMETHING NEW AND
exciting!

Take a minute with

CLARISSA PRITCHETT

Motivation is like bathing. You've got to do it every single day. ~ Zig Ziglar

Your body is the outer shell that protects the most intimate parts of your being. Your spirit and soul play a large part in forming your character to prepare for each day. Having inborn motivation to prepare is a blessing because external factors are unable to take it away. You need to be your biggest fan and there should be few things that you consider yourself unable to accomplish. Having confidence in God, yourself, and having internal motivation results in ongoing success and greater strides in the direction of your calling and destiny. When you look in the mirror each morning see an image of purpose. See someone who is hungry to achieve greatness with all God has equipped you with. By identifying with the reflection of who you are in Christ, pump yourself up to take time to plan, prepare, and persist even on the toughest days.

Affirmation: Motivation comes from within me.

How will you prepare today?

_____

_____

_____

_____

_____

_____

_____

_____

_____

_____

_____

_____

_____

_____

_____

_____

_____

_____

_____

_____

_____

_____

_____

_____

GIVE YOURSELF A FOOT

massage

Take a minute with
DEBORAH RIVERS DECOTEAU

You don't have to see the whole staircase, just take the first step. ~ Martin Luther King Jr

When we plan and prepare for our big, hairy, audacious goals, sometimes it can feel overwhelming. Looking at the big picture can sometimes leave us feeling like we are not moving forward or moving fast enough. This is when we should shift our method of preparation. Even though we keep the end result in mind, we take a step back from the big picture to focus on the task immediately in front of us. Preparing to succeed also means breaking big goals down into smaller, easier to conquer chunks. Then accomplishing these smaller chunks, piece by piece, gives us faster and more noticeable victories. This boosts our morale and encourages us to keep going. You know you're going to the top. "You don't have to see the whole staircase. Just take the first step" and see how great you feel. Then take another. And another.

Affirmation: I prepare to succeed by taking things one step at a time.

How will you prepare today?

_____

_____

_____

_____

_____

_____

_____

_____

_____

_____

_____

_____

_____

_____

_____

_____

_____

_____

_____

_____

CLOSE YOUR EYES AND *listen!*

Take a minute with
JISELLE ALLEYNE-CLEMENT

For everything that happens in life—there is a season, a right time for everything, every purpose under heaven. ~ Ecclesiastes 3:1

A major part of any preparation process is understanding the stage of the process we are in at any given moment. This requires deep analysis and self-awareness to ensure that our preparation process is aligned with our progress. When the preparation process is misaligned, the result is stagnancy. The word of God gives us the antidote to this problem. We are encouraged to *"understand the times and seasons that we are in, so we will know exactly what we should do..."* 1 Chronicles 12:32.

As we continue this journey of life, we are encouraged to walk in the accuracy of each season, by taking time to connect with our Heavenly Father. We must understand His timetable for our lives and let this knowledge guide our readiness to enter our new season.

Affirmation: I prepare accurately and walk in the fulfillment of every season in my life.

How will you prepare today?

_____

_____

_____

_____

_____

_____

_____

_____

_____

_____

_____

_____

_____

_____

_____

_____

_____

_____

_____

_____

YOU CAN DO THIS!

ENJOY A CUP OF HOT

Tea

Take a minute with
DR. KAREN MAXFIELD-LUNKIN

Then the LORD said to me, "Write my answer plainly on tablets, so that a runner can carry the correct message to others." ~ Habakkuk 2:2

Write the vision then envision yourself working the plan! This written vision is not only for those who read it to run with it but also a map and bridge for yourself. In the written vision/plan, prepare for the obstacles that may come along the way to the finish line or the next level. Prepare for the resistance in writing. Write the words of encouragement for yourself within the vision. Remind yourself that you are on a journey, and you are prepared for the roadblocks and detours. Write what your "bridge" looks like so when you arrive at the checkpoints you won't be fooled or detoured, and instead will easily cross over. Write the Blueprint for your B.R.I.D.G.E.. you will use to get beyond this issue. In the vision statement, prepare your mind for the plan of action for when obstacles arrive:

Be persistent

Reflect on your vision

Imagine yourself

Determine to push and Develop a...

Growth Mindset

Embracing the obstacles as friends, not failures.

Affirmation: I plan to succeed because I have a plan.

How will you prepare today?

_____

_____

_____

_____

_____

_____

_____

_____

_____

_____

_____

_____

_____

_____

_____

_____

_____

_____

_____

_____

WRITE THE VISION

WATCH A SHORT FUNNY *video*

Take a minute with
KARYN THOMPSON FARMER

'For I know the plans I have for you' - this is the Lord's declaration - 'plans for your welfare, not for disaster, to give you a future and a hope.' Jer 29:11 HCSB

Although the mantle, the calling, the assignment, and expectations of a leader can be both rewarding and daunting, it is joyous to know that God has declared that he knows the plans for our lives. If God knows the plans, then we as leaders need to embrace God's plans and perfect will by spending time and communication with God. His word promises that there are multiple plans for our lives. To receive the manifestation of God's plans for you for execution, it is important to lead with authority and be able to prepare:

P - *Pray*

R - *Record the Vision*

E - *Engage a 'Dream Team'*

P - *Position & Posture*

A - *Account for risks and mitigate*

R - *Ramp-up*

E - *Establish metrics and Execute*

Affirmation: I prepare to receive the manifestation of God's plans for me.

How will you prepare today?

_____

_____

_____

_____

_____

_____

_____

_____

_____

_____

_____

_____

_____

_____

_____

_____

_____

_____

_____

_____

_____

RELAX
YOUR
ENTIRE
BODY
and again

Take a minute with
NADIA MORALES

Call to me and I will answer you and tell you great and unsearchable things you do not know. ~ Jeremiah 33:3, NIV

Most of us have heard the quote, "if you fail to plan, you plan to fail." And perhaps, you have done your due diligence – you have a handful of plans that you try to stick to and execute.

Well, I have a question for you. Have you asked God to minister to you while you're planning out the next steps to get from Point A to Point B? Oftentimes, we write down ambitions and plans and just tell God we want it. There could also be days that we just give Him an FYI, albeit not on purpose – we are just too excited with what is possible because He has placed a desire in our hearts.

If you haven't yet, I encourage you to invite God in when you feel the need to go back to the drawing board. The knowledge of God gives us direction and peace, and His faithfulness carries us through.

Affirmation: My plans are decreed by the Lord. I will not fail.

How will you prepare today?

_____
_____
_____
_____
_____
_____
_____
_____
_____
_____
_____
_____
_____
_____
_____
_____
_____
_____
_____
_____
_____

TAKE A BREAK FROM

social media

Take a minute with
PATTI DENISE HENRY

The LORD himself goes before you and will be with you; he will never leave you nor forsake you. Do not be afraid; do not be discouraged. ~ Deuteronomy 31:8

Did you know that the Lord goes before us to set the stage for peace, victory, and great success? Understand that when preparation meets opportunity, success is sure to happen. One of the ways God prepares us is by tilling the soil of our hearts to prepare us to bear great fruit and yield a great harvest. He will also cleanse us, wash us, and purify us, so that we will be ready to serve Him in spirit and in truth. He renews our minds so that we walk not after the flesh, but after the Spirit. And He prepares us to be a sanctuary – a place that He can always abide by creating a habitation within us.

Affirmation: I have peace, victory, and great success because the Lord Himself prepares me.

How will you prepare today?

_____

_____

_____

_____

_____

_____

_____

_____

_____

_____

_____

_____

_____

_____

_____

_____

_____

_____

_____

_____

_____

_____

_____

COOL DOWN WITH A GLASS OF

water

Take a minute with
RONDA PARKS

And the LORD answered me, and said, Write the vision, and make it plain upon tables, that he may run that readeth it" ~ Habakkuk 2:2

Prepare yourself. Plan out what God would have you to do. Don't be discouraged. Don't allow anxiety in. Do not allow people to get in your way. In Habakkuk 2:2 it says "The LORD gave me this answer: 'Write down clearly on tablets what I reveal to you, so that it can be read at a glance.'" Follow what God has given you to do. Trust that God has not only given you the vision but and He has also prepared you for the tasks ahead of you. Do not give up. Do not back away. Continue to strive forward in all things.

Affirmation: I trust that God has prepared me for the vision He gave me.

How will you prepare today?

_____

_____

_____

_____

_____

_____

_____

_____

_____

_____

_____

_____

_____

_____

_____

_____

_____

_____

_____

_____

_____

_____

_____

DO EVERYTHING WITH HEART

You've prayed and prepared and now it is time to dodge every distraction and

Persist

LOOK IN THE MIRROR AND GIVE YOURSELF

a compliment

Take a minute with
ALLISON DENISE ARNETT

Finish what you start. ~ Unknown

You've had it up to here. And today kind of sucks. I get it. Anyone who says they don't have days like this is lying to themselves. Even Jesus, the Author and Finisher of our faith, had a rough day (see the Garden of Gethsemane) yet He still finished. Otherwise, how could we call Him the Finisher of our faith?

Today may be hard, "*but I have prayed [especially] for you [Your Name Here], that your faith [and confidence in God] may not fail; and you, once you have turned back again [to God], will strengthen and support your brothers [and sisters in the faith]." Luke 22:32 AMP*

Do not give up. Let God "*who began the good work within you, continue his work until it is finally finished on the day when Christ Jesus returns. Philippians 1:6 NLT* Stick it through and see what God will do.

Affirmation: I run on and God renews my strength.

How will you persist today?

_____

_____

_____

_____

_____

_____

_____

_____

_____

_____

_____

_____

_____

_____

_____

_____

_____

_____

_____

_____

_____

TIDY UP AND CLEAR OUT THE CLUTTER

around you

Take a minute with
CLARICE MAY CREGGER

No matter what comes your way, push harder than last time. ~ Unknown

God created you for such a time as this. Challenges and hurdles are designed to be hard but they were never meant to break you to the point of you giving up. Some challenges and hurdles in life may make you question if you are doing the right thing, but that's when you must trust God. Trust that He is using them to push you to be the person He created you to be. Push harder and know that you are made for this.

Affirmation: I will persevere no matter what because God is my strength and through Him I can do all things.

How will you persist today?

_____

_____

_____

_____

_____

_____

_____

_____

_____

_____

_____

_____

_____

_____

_____

_____

_____

_____

_____

_____

CREATE YOUR OWN SUNSHINE

WRITE FIVE THINGS YOU ARE GRATEFUL FOR

right now

Take a minute with
CLARISSA PRITCHETT

Persistence wears out resistance. ~ Unknown

Your ability to bypass potential distractions is profound. Persistence keeps you focused. Surround yourself with friends that support your commitment to your mission. Appreciate those special people who respect your drive and sense of purpose. Let doubts serve as sources of creativity for yourself. Use all obstacles as driving forces to guide you in finding solutions to problems and do not give up when one avenue of approach seems to be an uneven road or a dead end. Be proud that you were created by an all-mighty God with the heart of a fighter for your future. Remember that your ability to do great things comes from your firm belief that anything is possible through Christ who strengthens you.

Affirmation: Whenever I see that peer pressure or potential life problems are aiming to take me off course, I shut it down and I pray, prepare, and persist.

How will you persist today?

_____

_____

_____

_____

_____

_____

_____

_____

_____

_____

_____

_____

_____

_____

_____

_____

_____

_____

_____

_____

DO'NUT GIVE UP

Get up
AND TAKE
A GOOD
DEEP
STRETCH

Take a minute with
DEBORAH RIVERS DECOTEAU

When you get tired, learn to rest not quit. ~ Unknown

Burnout is real. It's not just in your head and it's not something you always need to try to just push through. If you don't take the tell-tale signs of burnout seriously, your body can shutdown leaving you unable to move forward. Sometimes the greatest thing you can do to keep pressing towards your goals is to pause. A pause is a temporary stop. Key word is temporary. Quitting is permanent and we can't do that. What you do in that pause is just as important as taking the pause itself. Make your pause purposeful by intentionally resting. Rest your body. Rest your mind. Rest your spirit. Just long enough to refresh and revive your energy and passion for the task. Then restart with a renewed spirit and persist until something positively exceptional happens.

Affirmation: I rest when I am tired. I do not quit.

How will you persist today?

_____

_____

_____

_____

_____

_____

_____

_____

_____

_____

_____

_____

_____

_____

_____

_____

_____

_____

_____

_____

_____

SMILE.
YEP THAT'S
IT!

just smile

Take a minute with

JISELLE ALLEYNE-CLEMENT

Deep calls to deep at the [thundering] sound of Your waterfalls; All Your breakers and Your waves have rolled over me. ~ Psalm 42:7

Life can sometimes feel like an obstacle course. Sometimes it feels like no amount of training can prepare you for the surprises of the uncharted terrains of life. It is at these times that we must dig deep into the reservoir of our souls and PULL. At these times, we may be surprised at the depths of our internal reservoir and our ability to refill, be refreshed, and have our souls revived. My friend, keep on PULLING, don't be afraid of exhausting your supply, for this supply is replenished by the inexhaustible resources of your Heavenly Father. He continuously refills our internal reservoir with living water, so as we PULL deep within, we are in fact pulling on HIM. Don't be distracted by other reservoirs beckoning you to come drink, be fiercely focused and persistent as you press into the deep.

Affirmation: I drink my fill from the river of life and I flourish and bloom like a well-watered garden.

How will you persist today?

_____
_____
_____
_____
_____
_____
_____
_____
_____
_____
_____
_____
_____
_____
_____
_____
_____
_____
_____
_____

HAVE A HEALTHY SNACK
or two!

Take a minute with
DR. KAREN MAXFIELD-LUNKIN

And now, dear brothers and sisters, one final thing. Fix your thoughts on what is true, and honorable, and right, and pure, and lovely, and admirable. Think about things that are excellent and worthy of praise. ~ Philippians 4:8 NLT

Have you ever struggled with not being present? You know, worried about the future or living in the blame, shame, and regret of the past? When in this place, we are distracted, on edge, and lack focus.

Push past the regret of your own past mistakes (shame) or reliving what someone else did to you in the past (blame). These two thought patterns have been called the lowest emotional frequencies next to death. At the other end of this spectrum in our heads, is worry or fear about the future.

Practice gratitude to persist beyond these mindsets. Gratitude is the anchor that pulls our thoughts out of the gutter of the past and the uncertainty of the future and anchors us to the present.

Affirmation: I am grateful for this present moment.

How will you persist today?

_____

_____

_____

_____

_____

_____

_____

_____

_____

_____

_____

_____

_____

_____

_____

_____

_____

_____

_____

_____

WATCH A SHORT INSPIRING *video*

Take a minute with
KARYN THOMPSON FARMER

Successful men and women keep moving. They make mistakes, but they do NOT quit. ~ Conrad Hilton

As a leader, you consistently need to speak and remind yourself and others about the power of persistence. Persistence is the need to press on, and not give up on your journey to achieving your goals. There are times when you may feel like giving up because your dreams appear to be too lofty and the obstacles you face seem too challenging to overcome. This is the point that determines who will push and press through until something happens.

Giving up and giving in is not an option. Perhaps you need to simply pause, regroup, and alter your course but do not abort your assignment. There is a blessing in your pressing. Your breakthrough is on the way. Keep moving and live F.R.E.E..

F - Faithful

R - Resilient

E - Extraordinary

E - Expecting

Affirmation: I live FREE and persist.

How will you persist today?

_____

_____

_____

_____

_____

_____

_____

_____

_____

_____

_____

_____

_____

_____

_____

_____

_____

_____

_____

_____

_____

_____

MUST

KEEP

GOING

WRITE OUT YOUR TO-DO LIST AND

prioritize it

Take a minute with
NADIA MORALES

And we know that in all things God works for the good of those who love him, who have been called according to his purpose. ~ Romans 8:28, NIV

Move. Act. Time to press forward.

Press forward with your eyes set to God.

Press forward with that spirit of excellence that He has put in your heart.

Press forward knowing that you are made in His likeness and that you will triumph because of His grace.

Press forward despite the obstacles that had set you back.

The challenge could be mental.

It could be physical.

But knowing that God has ordained you to a greater purpose means that your dream will come to pass.

Affirmation: My heart rests on this truth: with His grace, I will triumph.

How will you persist today?

_____

_____

_____

_____

_____

_____

_____

_____

_____

_____

_____

_____

_____

_____

_____

_____

_____

_____

_____

_____

_____

_____

_____

BREATHE IN SOME LAVENDAR

essential oil

Take a minute with
PATTI DENISE HENRY

Yet in all these things we are more than conquerors through Him who loved us. ~ Romans 8:37

Do not lose heart. Instead, persist and prevail. Understand that even when we are pressed on every side, we are not crushed. We may be perplexed, but not in despair. We may be persecuted but not abandoned. Struck down, but not destroyed. Thank God that we are overcomers and more than conquerors. And because of this we can run this race with patience knowing that in the end we will hear God say, "Well done, my good and faithful servant." Knowing that in the end, we win!

Affirmation: I run with patience knowing that in the end we win.

How will you persist today?

_____

_____

_____

_____

_____

_____

_____

_____

_____

_____

_____

_____

_____

_____

_____

_____

_____

_____

_____

_____

_____

ASK YOURSELF WHAT YOU NEED RIGHT NOW

and get it

Take a minute with
RONDA PARKS

But as for you, be strong and do not give up, for your work will be rewarded." ~ 2 Chronicles 15:7

Do you feel like giving up? Wait! Before you answer that question, seek God's word. Seek the instruction He has given us in 2 Chronicles 15:7 – *"be strong and do not give up, for your work will be rewarded."* God will reward you for your work. As instructed in Galatians 6:9 "let us not become tired of doing good; for if we do not give up, the time will come when we will reap the harvest." Do not give up. Keep pressing forward. This race was designed just for you and so you be confident that you can do it. God has ordered your steps and He will guide you through. Be strong and do not give up.

Affirmation: Because I do not give up, I will be rewarded.

How will you persist today?

_____

_____

_____

_____

_____

_____

_____

_____

_____

_____

_____

_____

_____

_____

_____

_____

_____

_____

_____

_____

_____

_____

Meet the Authors

ALLISON DENISE ARNETT

Christian Minister & Teacher • Author Brand Strategist & Publisher

Allison Denise is an Author Brand Strategist & Publisher, 12x Best Selling Author, International Speaker, and Award-Winning Graphic Designer of beautiful boss books and author brands through her biz Brand It Beautifully™. A servant leader at heart and an eclectic, creative soul, she seeks to help others stir up their dormant gifts while transforming lives. Every book she authors or event she hosts is designed to influence Christian Women in Business to own who they are, say what you have to say, and walk in your divine feminine power. God has blessed her to empower you to do this in two ways:

Publishing & Design
Ready to publish your book and build a legacy-leaving, influential author brand? God has gifted Allison with Creative Vision to help you share your message with the world via books.

Spiritual Empowerment
Allison Denise writes books and produces podcasts to empower Christian women to stand in their God-designed feminine power in their minds, ministries, and in the marketplace.

Connect with Allison: www.BrandItBeautifully.ccom

CLARICE MAY CREGGER

Clarice May Cregger (AKA "Coach Claire") was born and raised in Olongapo City, Philippines. She currently resides in Albuquerque, NM with her husband, Richard Torres. Clarice is an Amazon best-selling author, publishing her first book in 2020 as a co-author of "Heart of God for Her: 45 Day Devotional – Revealing God's Love for His Leading Ladies. But in April 2021, she published her very own book called "Broken But Beautifully Made 4 Steps to finding beauty in your brokenness". Clarice is a creative entrepreneur, specializing in life transformation coaching, professional photography with her Claire May Photography & Design LLC business, she's also an international speaker and motivator and she founded the International Women's Empowerment Group called "Broken But Beautifully Made LLC". As a certified life coach, she thankfully utilizes her craft of transformational coaching with a keen focus on breaking harmful patterns and overcoming guilt and shame. With a compelling backstory of her own, Clarice is very passionate about helping women of all ages find their voice, strength, and beauty while overcoming past hurts. With a backdrop of faith in God, Clarice helps women and anyone in need fulfill their God-given purpose in life.

CLARISSA PRITCHETT

Clarissa Pritchett, M.P.H., is an Integrative Nutrition Health Coach, Empowerment Speaker, Author, Entrepreneur, and Army Medical Service Corps Officer. Clarissa is a wife and mom to three beautiful boys. Clarissa is passionate about health and wellness and has served numerous clients over the past 20 years. She has a Bachelor's degree in Health Education, a Master's Degree in Public Health Nutrition, and numerous certifications in the fitness and nutrition field. She is an online health coach and self-care coach who also mentors women to start online businesses while promoting Sisterhood, Self-Care, and Service to those in need. She loves to encircle and uplift women to live healthy lives. She has written numerous recipe and health guide eBooks. She is a sought-after speaker and resilience instructor for the military, wellness companies, and local churches to where she shares her story of overcoming health/life challenges and motivates women with their health and life goals. Clarissa is a short, sweet, and spicy mixed salad sistah that keeps it real, raw, and organic about how she overcame many health challenges and body issues. Overall, her favorite things in life are Jesus, family, friends, cooking and eating food, especially tacos, donuts, and chocolate!

Learn more and connect with Clarissa on IG and Facebook @ClarissaHealthCoach or on her website at www.ClarissaPritchett.com and Treat yourself to some healthy self-care at www.EmpirePoshQueen.com

DEBORAH RIVERS DECOTEAU

Deborah Rivers Decoteau is a 3x Best Selling Author, Wellness Director, and Caribbean Carnival Costume Designer and Band Leader. A native of Trinidad and Tobago, she has dedicated her life to bringing awareness to her culture via singing, dancing, and writing. It is her life's work to empower women to wellness and to live a life by God's design. Deborah is a mother of five and is affectionately known by her grandchildren as Little G. When she is not adding building blocks to her legacy, you will find her in Houston, Texas crafting to keep her creative ideas flowing.

JISELLE ALLEYNE-CLEMENT

Jiselle Alleyne-Clement is a professional of many hats. She is an Academic Librarian, Educator, and Researcher. She received her MLIS in Library Science from Dalhousie University, Canada. She also holds an MA in Leadership Studies from the University of Guelph, Canada, and she is currently reading for her Ph.D. in Gender Studies at the University of the West Indies, focusing on Female Leadership Development in Caribbean Organizations.

Jiselle is the lead Empowerment Speaker, Vision Coach, and Mentor, through her consultancy, 'Pearls of Great Price Empowerment Services', a consultancy developed for faith-based women.

The empowerment programs offered through her consultancy are geared to help women manage the transitions in their lives and will treat with topics such as, but not limited to:
Competencies for Seamless Transition Management
Establishing Healthy and Productive SHE Team Cultures
SHE Leadership Development
Developing a Resilience Mindset

Jiselle believes that every woman must be given access to this type of development where she can, in turn, lead within her sphere of influence.

DR. KAREN MAXFIELD-LUNKIN

Dr. Karen Maxfield-Lunkin is a best-selling, award winning, literary coach and visionary author, an educational entrepreneur with nearly years of experience as a teacher, mentor, school principal, professor, parent-coach and educational advocate. Described as a thought leader and innovator, Dr. Karen's mission is to "guide people through writing to uncover to discover and finally recover their God-given gifts and talents buried deep within them."

Dr. Karen enjoys inspiring future authors to write and publish. A guest lecturer and adjunct university professor, and involved in numerous community initiatives, including chairwoman of the board of directors for an African Diaspora group in Austin, Texas. An ordained minister, Dr. Karen is also the founder of Bridge Kingdom Ministries, a nonprofit organization with the mission to actively explore opportunities for business and entrepreneurial connection; Improve educational methods to recognize the treasures already in our possession, by learning and activating Kingdom principles. Bridging Africans and African Americans to face and heal from the past traumas from our ancestral past with the "twist" of approaching the past with forgiveness, and creative determination to reframe present conditions through the lens of God's Word.

Residing in Austin, Texas with Michael, her husband of thirty-three years, they have three grown children, and two rescue dogs.

KARYN THOMPSON FARMER

Karyn Thompson Farmer is an entrepreneur as a Founding Partner of Twelvesat12 LLC, a niche management consulting firm. Prior to becoming an entrepreneur, Karyn was a senior leader in corporate America for large-scale cybersecurity delivery teams. Karyn is a Hampton University, Math/Comp Science, graduate where she was initiated into Delta Sigma Thera Sorority, Inc.

Karyn is a sought after speaker for Women's Empowerment; she teaches and provides women with tools to achieve financial freedom through entrepreneurship and embracing their powerful voice to live F.R.E.E - Faithful | Resilient | Extraordinary | Expecting. She is a Amazon #1 Best Selling Author. She co-moderates weekly Clubhouse Rooms ~ 'Sisters Supporting Sisters' and UBW 'Business-Minded Friday.' In addition, Karyn co-hosts a radio broadcast called, 'Sundays with Twelvesat12,' with her business partner.

Karyn is a leader that has blazed trails for women of color through her innovative approach to entrepreneurship, vision casting and team building. She is an advocate for youth academic enrichment. Karyn leverages her technical and creative design skills to expose boys and girls to various STEM courses and camps she establishes, designs and delivers.

Karyn is a resilient and relational leader that loves the Lord and stands on His promises. Karyn lives in Maryland with her family.

NADIA MORALES

Nadia Morales is a brand and web designer who empowers and equips female course creators to serve and change the world. She became a corporate drop-out when she went out of her comfort zone to find what gives her joy. When you can't find her in front of her computer, she's either recreating recipes online, reading a few books on Kindle, or playing with her cat, Tommy.

Follow her on Instagram @hanancreatives or reach out to her for partnerships at nadia@hanancreatives.com

PATTI DENISE HENRY

A native of the Island of Trinidad & Tobago, Patti is internationally recognized as a Minister, Psalmist, Teacher, Hospice Chaplain, Family & Bereavement Counselor, Best Selling Author, and Prolific Speaker. She is also known as "A Prophetic Worshiper" as her sound in the earth impacts the heart and minds of all who come into contact with her ministry.

Patti Henry uses biblical insight along with life experiences to help you to identify "The Holes in Your Soul" and provide the necessary tools to transform you into a "Beautiful Soul".

She is the Founder & President of Patti Denise International Ministries, The Soul Coach, and Sisters, Let's Keep Talking! Patti is humbled by the call that God has placed on her life and is very passionate about her purpose which is to multiply disciples for Christ and to function as a Soul Coach where she motivates others to live before they die. She is indeed a Servant Leader for such a time as this.

Contact Patti at www.IAmTheSoulCoach.com

RONDA PARKS

Ronda R. Parks is a Washington, DC native who currently resides in Maryland. For the past 21 years, she has worked as an Accounting Associate at the Center for Science in the Public Interest (CSPI). Parks is an active member of New Friendship Baptist Church, where she is also First Lady. Her dedication and involvement over the Women's Ministry and other empowering events have allowed her to have an influential impact in the lives of others, leading to her being awarded The Deborah C. Offer Bulgin Women of Virtue Walking in Excellence Award for the Ministry category in 2019. She is a strong believer in prayer and standing firm on your Faith and has a lifelong passion for serving the women and children around her. Ronda R. Parks loves the Lord with all her heart, and in her words "God handpicked me because I would not have picked myself".

www.ingramcontent.com/pod-product-compliance
Lightning Source LLC
Chambersburg PA
CBHW051856090426
42811CB00003B/350